FINDING YOUR IDEAL PARTNER

FINDING YOUR IDEAL PARTNER

8 STEPS TO THE RELATIONSHIP YOU REALLY WANT

Karin Heinitz

Karin Heinitz © Copyright 2011

New Yoga Publications, Whitstable, U.K.

ISBN-13: 978-1456516109 ISBN-10: 1456516108 CreateSpace

Content

FOREWORD

There are times in one's life when the whole world seems to walk around in couples holding hands; when one is invited to a party and can't bear the thought of going out alone again; when the woman with the two children at the supermarket check-out seems to look with condescending pity at one's shopping basket with the small tin of peas and the half-sized loaf. In short, there are times when being single seems to mean loneliness and exclusion from normal life.

Not being in a relationship can seem like a self-inflicted wound open for everyone to see. We may feel guilty, ashamed, outcast and an embarrassment to our friends who, of course, all have partners. We want one too and we want one now, full stop!

So we think we've got to do something. Our friends advise us to answer lonely hearts ads or place one ourselves after they have unsuccessfully tried to match us with another unfortunate single whom we detested at first sight. Of course, we have already tried everything from the chat rooms of internet web sites for singles to going to evening classes to joining the Ramblers Association, from visiting the local Singles Club to getting counselling. Still no partner in sight.

No matter if you continue searching or decide to stay at home from now on, doing the Eight Steps should help you not just to bring a partner into your life, but the partner you really want.

People who have done the Eight Steps got married, or found a temporary partner if that was what they wanted. Some discovered that being in a relationship was not really a priority at that time in their lives, and one fell in love with a woman after years of trying relationships with men.

Healers and shamans have used the principles applied in the Eight Steps for thousands of years. And indeed, everyone I know who has seriously and honestly tried them has had success.

INTRODUCTION

What keeps us from finding our ideal partner and forces us to repeat unsatisfactory relationship patterns? Only one thing: we have emotional baggage which gets in the way. This baggage can be removed with some effort, some patience and with determination in only eight steps.

The Eight Steps are a technique that is easy to apply yet one cannot apply it mechanically. Work with the Eight Steps means working with the whole of you. You need to use your awareness, your beliefs, your consciousness, your body, and your intent. But above all you will need to harness your desire for what you want and be truly ready and willing to receive it.

You have to be unconditionally prepared to get what you want right now for the Eight Steps to make your dream of an ideal partner come true.

Yet when we dream of something we are sometimes worried that 'the dream come true' could turn out to be a nightmare. This is particularly so where relationships are concerned. We dream that we will no longer be lonely, that we'll be happy and everything in our lives will be better with a partner. Yet deep down we may also fear that our lives will change, that we will lose our freedom, that we may choose the wrong partner. Therefore it is important to find out what our fantasies and expectations are, and not just those we enjoy thinking about but also those darker ones which lurk in the back of our mind.

The first chapter shows what to look for, how to deal with those anxieties and how to prepare yourself.

> Once you are sure that having your ideal partner in your life right now is what you really want begin work with the EIGHT STEPS.

The Eight Steps are based on a specific method which I call Embodied Visualisation. The exercises will engage your body as well as your mind, and focus your intent on the goal you desire.

The way in which the gathering of will and desire will bring your ideal partner into your life is similar to how you bring other things into your life. What shapes our experience of life are our beliefs and desires. If you want to know more about this concept I suggest you read Jane Roberts, The Nature of Reality – a Seth Book. It doesn't matter, however, if you understand or believe in this concept, you don't even have to believe that the Eight Steps will work, just open yourself to the possibility that they might and take them.

The way in which we experience the world and our relationships is shaped by the beliefs which we hold about ourselves and the world and the assumptions we make, many of them subconsciously. Once we are in a relationship we will encounter these beliefs and assumptions as reality. Some of them may manifest as conflicts and challenges. These can be difficult to navigate but are also opportunities for change and growth and for deepening your ideal relationship.

To begin a relationship is one thing, yet to maintain it over years, to keep it close, intimate and fresh is another. This demands that we face the difficult aspects in our partner and in ourselves, and that we get to know each other on an ever deeper level.

In the second half of this book I have shared some key thoughts about the nature of relationships which you might want to meditate. I also make suggestions for resolving conflicts. They can help you to steer through difficulties as they will occur in even the most harmonious relationship. These thoughts are gathered from my experience with my friends, with psychotherapy clients and, of course, from relating to my partner. They are insights which have proved to be an excellent foundation on which to build.

The summary on the last page gives a quick overview of the essentials of this book and can serve as a reminder, once you've got down to working with the Eight Steps.

OBSTACLES TO FINDING YOUR IDEAL PARTNER

BELIEFS

The beliefs which we hold about the world shape the way in which we perceive it. If I believe that I can generally trust people I will take a let down as something that unfortunately happens occasionally. If however, I believe that 'you can't trust anybody' then I will see a let down as a confirmation that I am right in not trusting. The more suspicious I become the more reasons I will find not to trust. I lose my ability to discriminate and, in the worst case, become paranoid and have persecutory fantasies.

A belief is an assumption I make about myself and about the world. In childhood we learn what to believe from parents and other important adults, from peers, from the internet, from TV, books and other media. We also create beliefs ourselves by trying to make sense of the world with the little information we have got as children. Most of these beliefs we regard as truth far beyond childhood. They pop into our minds and we take their validity for granted without questioning them or checking them against our experience. Our experience seems to confirm our beliefs.

We actually tend to overlook what doesn't fit into our belief system. At the time when we accepted the beliefs they were probably useful or at least we were not in a position to judge them. However, many of them maybe outdated and no longer appropriate for the adult we are now nor for the world we live in.

Take Julia who has a law degree and used to be a solicitor. She does an MA part-time while holding a job in which she often works more than 30 hours per week. Julia already has another MA and is employed below her qualification as a secretary. She often speaks of herself as stupid and lazy. She was called that by her primary school teacher and by her mother when in fact she was bored at school and shy. Now she finds it difficult to value her achievements and even to acknowledge that she is working hard. She believes that her degree can't be worth much if a stupid person like her can do it, and really, she shouldn't take a day off, go out, or do something that is not work. She thinks nobody could want her as a partner. Her beliefs make her life a misery.

Although we are often not aware of our beliefs that doesn't mean they are unconscious. Julia knows that she believes herself to be stupid and lazy. Yet she thinks it is true despite the evidence of her daily reality.

If we listen to what we think is the truth about ourselves we can find out what our beliefs are. We can question their validity and if some of them hinder us in getting what we want from life we'd better find beliefs that work for us.

After all, beliefs are just thoughts, words in our heads, nothing else. With them we are trying to explain the world to ourselves. Yet if they are contradicting reality as much as Julia's did they need to be reformulated.

> Fortunately, beliefs about reality are not reality.
> We can change them.

**some beliefs
about the WORLD
that make it difficult
to find your ideal partner**

THERE ARE NO SUITABLE MEN/WOMEN OF MY AGE AVAILABLE

Although it might appear as if everybody you know in your age group is either in a relationship or obviously unsuitable this doesn't matter at all. Remind yourself that there are people around whom you don't know yet and one of them longs to meet you.

Open yourself to the possibility that there is at least one person who is right and available for you.

MEN ARE BASTARDS
WOMEN ARE BITCHES

Generalisations like this are never true and you know it, even if up till now your experience confirms this belief.

All you need is
to meet *one* person who is different - never mind the rest.

But it would probably help to find out what makes you fear or hate the opposite or your own gender so much.

ALL RELATIONSHIPS BREAK DOWN
EVENTUALLY

Again, this may be your personal experience. After all, so far your relationships didn't work out. Maybe your parents and friends are divorced or in bad relationships. None of this is important.

What *is* important is that for *you* it is possible to be in a relationship which will not only be enduring but also very special and right for you.

**some beliefs
about YOURSELF
that make it difficult
to find your ideal partner**

When I talk with people who long for a partner but are single or seem to have a pattern of painful and dissatisfying relationships I ask them why they think that happens. There are of course unique reasons for every person.

Then I ask what they think about relationships and how they feel about themselves. Often one or more of the following thoughts are mentioned. On a closer look these thoughts which seem so true to the one who thinks them can be recognised as beliefs.

- I am too old/fat/ugly/bad... for anybody to love me

- If I commit myself to one person I might miss out

- I am far too difficult for anybody to put up with

- When I am close to someone I become who they want me to be

- I lose my independence when I fall in love

- I find it difficult to be intimate with people

- Nobody could possibly understand me

- I am too boring, nobody finds me interesting

- I am unattractive

- I am too sensitive

- I am uncomfortable with having sex

- I will get hurt again

If any of the above sentences feel familiar you are probably afraid of being in a relationship. If you are afraid of being in a relationship you will find partners who confirm your fears and beliefs which then become a self-fulfilling prophesy.

You need to work on changing these beliefs even though you think that they are true.

Open yourself to the possibility that they might not be true and reformulate them.

Reformulation

Ask yourself what you would be scared of in a relationship. Make a list of at least eight negative thoughts you have about yourself, and eight about being in a relationship. Then reformulate each belief turning it into a positive statement. This is not the same as what is called 'Positive Thinking'.

Imagine that you believe that you don't deserve to be loved. If anybody told you that you do deserve it, would you believe them? If you believe something strongly, trying to persuade yourself that the opposite is true will not be acceptable to your mind – you know that black isn't white. Positive thinking is insulting to your mind.

Forget about 'Positive Thinking', just think and remember that if you are aware of a negative thought *as a thought* you won't mistake it for reality and so it cannot dominate you.

Allow for the possibility that reality could be different to what you think and believe.

Reformulation of your beliefs is easy because they are most often generalised statements. To create a belief that works better for you do not turn it into its opposite but formulate it as an alternative possibility.

EXAMPLE 1

"Nobody will want me because I am too boring."

Reformulation:

• I could find somebody who loves me just the way I am.

• I might meet someone who finds the way I am just right.

EXAMPLE 2

"I have difficulties being intimate with people."

Reformulation:

• There could be someone who will help me overcome my difficulties with intimacy

• There could be someone whose needs for intimacy are a perfect match to mine.

Whenever you catch yourself thinking the negative belief be aware that it is just a thought and replace it with the reformulated one. Sometimes this can be difficult particularly when those negative beliefs have been entertained for a very long time and are deeply ingrained. In that case it might be useful to ask an experienced psychotherapist or counsellor for help in changing them.

You need to reach a state in which you can say

> Now I am ready to begin a relationship.

This does not mean that you have to have conquered all your fears or changed all your negative beliefs. You may still be afraid but as long as you can say *I want it anyway* everything is OK.

> A relationship can also be an opportunity to
> overcome your fears
> with the help of your partner.

You may find that you don't want a relationship right now...

Fear of a relationship does not just result from negative beliefs. You may want a close relationship but it may not be right for you at this time in your life. If you find yourself reluctant to follow the suggestions, to invest the time and energy necessary, then consider the possibility that something else might be more important right now.

A friend of mine had for a long time thought about doing a training course. She knew it would be very hard work, it would take up all of her time, and she was afraid of exposing herself and failing. She also felt lonely and longed for a partner, and this had gone on for a long time. She felt that not having a partner held her back in all areas of her life. Eventually she decided to do the Eight Steps. She reformulated the negative beliefs she held about relationships. In this process however, she discovered that she had focused on being lonely in order not to have to think about the training course.

Four years later, after she had finished the training course, she did the Eight Steps again and 6 months after that she found the man she now lives with.

If you find yourself in a similar situation this should give you peace of mind. At least for the time being you can stop worrying about relationships and get on with what is really important for you right now.

There are also people who live satisfying and fulfilling lives without a partner and who would not achieve this in an intimate relationship. This is rare and it might not be easy to admit because everything around us is geared to coupledom.

However, if after honest exploration of your desires you come to the conclusion that for now a close and permanent partner would rather be an inconvenience than an enrichment of your life, accept it.

You can make your life rich in many ways and be proud of it.

EIGHT STEPS
TO
YOUR IDEAL RELATIONSHIP

You have decided that you are ready. Now you can begin to create your ideal relationship. Enjoy the process and approach it playfully.

You need a quiet space where you will not be disturbed for an hour. You may not always need that much time, or sometimes an hour may not be enough. There is no correct time span, let your concentration be the measure.

Step 1

EMBODYING A DIFFERENT YOU

Being in your ideal relationship will change the way you feel about yourself, new aspects of you will develop, others may recede. One could say that the person you will be in your ideal relationship is different to the person you are now. In this first exercise you will familiarise yourself with the person you could be. How we feel in our bodies is a good indicator for our general state of being. If we feel good we will also feel good in our body, if we don't our body doesn't feel good either. We embody who we are.

Imagine that you already are in your ideal relationship. Everything is just as you want it to be. Now you have a quiet moment to yourself. Become aware how you feel your body. It may feel warm or light, buzzing or radiant, calm or solid. Your body may feel relaxed and alert, it may feel more alive.

Give attention to every part of your body from top to toe, and explore the sensations you feel.

> The way we feel our bodies is
> the way we feel who we are.

Give yourself time to become aware how the new you could feel and, if you can, find a way of expressing this new sense of yourself in your everyday life through your body language.

Step 2

VISUALISING A DIFFERENT LIFE

When we imagine what it would be like to be with our beloved we tend to dream about the general picture. This exercise should help you to go into the details which give you information of all the things that may be important to you.

Imagine yourself together with your ideal partner. Choose an everyday situation or a special moment. Visualise your images as detailed as possible with colours, sounds, environment, time of day, time of year. Let your body participate as if you were totally there. Create the situation exactly as you would like it to be. Now become aware how you feel in this situation. What does your body feel like, what is your mood, what are your thoughts? Are you satisfied with how you feel in body and mind?

Now look at your partner. What sort of person is s/he? What do you know about her/him? Do you want to ask her/him about something? Listen inwardly for answers. See and feel your partner relating to you in a way that responds to who you truly are, to what you need.

Use the images and the bodily feelings to sense what is important for you.

If you don't feel totally comfortable, something is still amiss. Change the scene until your body feels really comfortable and good.

Write down what you visualised and felt.

Step 3

DEFINING YOUR RELATIONSHIP

After practicing Embodied Visualisation you are now ready to define what form the ideal relationship should take for you. Take a sheet of paper, copy the sentence 'This is my ideal ....' and fill in the gap.

You could write 'partner'. Yet this is not really specific enough. What you may really want to say could be 'This is my ideal life partner', 'This is my ideal lover', or 'This is my ideal husband/wife', or 'This is the ideal man/woman for me to live' with. Decide whether you want a lover, husband, wife, live-in partner, somebody who is your partner in life but doesn't live with you, or something else like 'my ideal intimate friend'.

Think very carefully about the form that your ideal relationship should have, and find words that are absolutely right for you.

Don't write what you think you should want. After all, you might have to live with your choice.

You wouldn't be too happy if you found yourself married and living together when in your heart of hearts you'd rather live on your own and have a loving companion with you over the weekend.

And if you want a family and a home an ardent lover who nevertheless guards his or her own space and time and doesn't want children will not fulfil your desire.

Step 4

DESCRIBE YOUR IDEAL PARTNER

Once you have decided what sort of relationship suits you best, write down what you want this person to be like. In order to do this, draw on the second step.

This is an opportunity to be as honest to yourself and as outrageous as you possibly can. It is not a time for political correctness or for pleasing your parents, impressing your friends or bolstering your self-image.

> Describe the person
> who would truly enrich your life.

Nobody else will have to see what you write unless you want to. Write what your *ideal* would be, nothing less will do.

For inspiration look at the example on page 68.

You may want to follow the categories in the example and also invent categories of your own. Write down as many qualities as you can think of, and again be as specific and accurate as possible. You may need a couple of pages or more.

A woman found that in her initial description she had focussed on qualities which when she read through them again she recognized to be her own. That made her think about the different *things that a partner could bring into her life, the qualities that she would find stimulating, surprising and exciting, and that she hadn't even known she desired.*

Work on Step 5 tomorrow.

Step 5

REVIEWING AND CHANGING -

More Visualisation and Embodiment

Go over your list again. Repeat step 2, the visualisation and embodiment exercise. You could include situations where you as a couple meet other people like family or friends. You could even imagine having a disagreement. Fill in as many details as possible and take care that you feel in the situation as you would like to feel. You have the power to create the situation as you want it.

Review your list.

Repeat this process until you find that your list is complete or you get bored with it. This usually takes from a couple of days to a week. Work on your list for no longer than a week, three or four days generally seem to be sufficient.

Step 6
STATING YOUR INTENT

It is very possible that you will get what you ask for. Unfortunately we sometimes want something that isn't particularly good for us although we don't know that before we get it. Or we don't ask for something which is really important because we don't know that it is important. Our conscious mind isn't of much help here, but our unconscious mind has a hand in creating what we want. However, we need to tell it what we want in terms that are clear and unmistakable.

Therefore, after you have repeated reviewing your list and are really satisfied with it, write underneath

This or something better will now come into my life in a harmonious and satisfying way.

Now...

Sign it, date it and put it away.

If you would rather use different words find those that feel right for you. But keep the term 'this or something better'. The term 'harmonious and satisfying' is meant to ensure that you get into your ideal relationship with as much ease as possible.

Step 7

AFFIRMING YOUR INTENT

Take a fresh sheet of paper. Write:

I, …….., am now ready and willing to let my ……………….. into my life.

In the first gap write the name by which you are known, in the second write the words you have chosen to describe your relationship (lover, husband, wife, loving companion, live-in partner, etc.) If you don't like the sentence above, find one that suits you better. What you do in writing this sentence is telling the Universe that you are ready to receive what you have asked for. This is what the sentence has to convey.

Repeat the sentence about 20 times or as long as you feel your desire and determination while writing it. You are giving out a message, and you want it to reach the person it is meant for, no matter where they may be. One of my clients who lives in Scotland found his love in France.

Write the sentence 20 times every day for at least two weeks.

Step 8

LETTING GO

After having written the sentence 20 times every day for at least two weeks but no more than four weeks, you have given out a very strong message. Now trust that this message will reach the person it is meant for. There is nothing else you need to do, just get on with your life and forget about the whole thing.

NOTHING ELSE TO DO?

NOTHING ELSE TO DO!

After I had done a less elaborate version of the exercises I didn't forget about it. My life seemed to open up and I met quite a few new people - which was already a considerable change to my former experience - but none of them seemed even remotely to be 'the one'. For four months I was disappointed, frustrated, and cynical about the assumption that my mind could get me what I wanted. Then I really did forget about it and let go, but angrily.

Nevertheless, about five months later I came together with my partner. I had met him for the first time four weeks after I had finished the Eight Steps. I just hadn't realised that he was the one because he didn't fulfil some of the requirements I had laid down in my description. After we got together, however, I found that he was the 'something better'.

RELATIONSHIPS –

SOME THOUGHTS TO MEDITATE ON

> We 'have' relationships but
> *relating* is something we *do*

We regard relationship as something we 'have' or 'don't have' like we have or don't have a car. We forget that a relationship only exists because we are relating – and relating is something *we do*.

The quality of relationships depends on how partners relate to each other and on their awareness of their way of relating.

A relationship without honest and intimate relating is no relationship at all but a charade.

> ‘Being interested’ in someone is not the
> same as *taking* an interest in them

What does it mean to be ‘interested in someone’? Does it mean fancying them, seeing them as a potential partner or taking a real *interest* in them?

These are, of course, not exclusive. Yet without taking a real interest in the other person your meeting will be all about you and not a good start for a relationship.

Taking an interest is not the same as checking the other out to see whether they fit your requirements.

Instead, you might want to know about their current life situation, about their desires, dreams, hopes, concerns. Think about what you would like another person to be interested in when they meet you for the first time.

If you are nervous you may try putting on your best face in order to impress the other person. As a result you may find yourself talking too much instead of giving your full attention to the other and taking a real interest in them.

If you are shy you may find yourself struggling for things to say. Yet why not think about things to ask instead of things to say – thus showing your interest in the other?

> **If two people begin a relationship they both want it to work – despite appearances**

If one partner is unhappy in the relationship, if one is frightened, it is very likely that the other has similar feelings.

You can safely assume that a serious partner's basic interest is to relate well to you, to love and be loved, and to continue the relationship. You both may be clumsy in expressing this, you may both get things wrong but as long as you acknowledge your partner's basic good intent despite appearances, you have a good chance of solving any conflict that comes your way.

> As we change, learn, grow so our
> relationship changes and grows

If you have a fixed image of who your partner is or ought to be, if you insist that your partner fits or grows into your image of them and don't value the real person which changes and grows in her/his own way and time, then the relationship cannot grow and becomes stale.

A relationship is ideal when partners can be themselves in every way and feel loved and respected anyway. If my partner can accept me with my idiosyncrasies and limitations, then I might be able to face them myself without defensiveness and chose whether to change or not.

A partner who can give feedback about what the other does without making that into a judgement about their value as a human being can be a wonderful help.

A relationship is not a finished product

Relationships are sustained through an ongoing process of relating. If one partner stops relating to the other and cuts off the relationship is suspended.

It can only be resumed when both partners are prepared to acknowledge, reflect on and discuss what is happening.

This can be an opportunity to learn more about the way we relate, and can help us to relate more deeply.

> ## Similarities between partners are delightful – differences are enriching

You and your partner may be similar in many respects. You may have similar values, similar interests or hobbies, similar ways of approaching most situations. Yet if there were only similarities between partners it would be as if they were relating to their own mirror image.

There will be differences and some of them may not be apparent at the beginning because we tend to first focus on the similarities.

If both partners suppress differences for fear that the other will respond badly, they will also feel resentment that neither can be who s/he really is.

Differences show you that life can be approached in other ways than those you are familiar with and therefore can be a source of surprise and of new discoveries.

They will enrich your relationship if you are open to them. If there weren't any differences you would probably be bored very quickly.

Even if someone seems to be your 'perfect' partner, you will find out that they have some habits that irritate you.

You are tidy and punctual while they have to search for the car keys every time you want to go out.

You want to go out spontaneously but your partner first needs to tidy up and wash the dishes before they are comfortable leaving.

They laugh about something that you find horrific and upsetting.

They always let their dirty cups stand around.

No partner is 'perfect' as such, and there will be some ways of behaving that just won't go away, even though you have complained, admonished, got upset.

You just have to live with it, I'm afraid. Accept it and remember that you will probably also have some habits that really irritate your partner.

> ## Intimacy can be expressed through sex but not created through it

Intimacy is an elusive concept. The word derives from the Latin 'intimus' meaning the innermost, deepest, most familiar. For the Romans 'intimus' signified a very good friend, someone close, loved and trusted. It was only much later that the term came to have sexual connotations.

Intimacy is what we feel when we know and deeply trust another person. By definition, we cannot be intimate with people we don't know.

Today 'being intimate' with somebody is just another phrase for having sex but sexual 'intimacy' does not imply that there is inner closeness between two people.

If we want to create an intimate relationship we have to give it time, get to know the other and let ourselves be known. Sexual attraction and sleeping together can help but they can also become a substitute or even a means of avoiding real intimacy.

Relating with our whole self

Many of us have not learnt to relate in an open and honest way. We don't believe that somebody could stay with us and love us if they really knew our deepest feelings, our hidden pains and shortcomings.

We put on a face that seems to make ourselves acceptable and conceal parts of ourselves that we think are not.

So, there we have two people who relate only from one part of themselves and hide another. It may take a lot of time until there is enough trust to reveal more. Yet only if we relate with our whole self.

> **If one partner has to give up a part of themselves both partners lose out**

Sharing interests is an important aspect of being a couple. Yet there will also be interests that one or the other partner doesn't want to share in because they may not find them appealing. Just because you enjoy a particular activity doesn't mean that your partner has to.

However, if these interests are important for you, you need to find space and time to pursue them no matter how your partner reacts.

If you feel that you have to give up something you enjoy because of your partner you will probably feel deprived and resentful.

'You make me feel...'

No, your partner doesn't *make* you feel anything.

You feel in response to what happens around you, and your response is coloured by what you believe and by the mood you are in. How you interpret what you are feeling is your responsibility.

I may feel frustrated when my partner wants to be alone and I want his company, but I need not feel rejected just because we have different needs at this point in time.

Only if you believe that your partner doesn't care about you, will you feel hurt. Most of the time your partner doesn't want to hurt you but to protect her/himself or even protect you.

If your partner does something you find difficult to cope with tell them – without blaming them for how you feel.

Don't treat me like this ...

If you feel treated wrongly in a relationship you have the obligation to yourself and your partner to say so. You have to let your partner know that something is wrong for you.

If you are afraid of asserting yourself you need to consider whether it feels better to suffer for standing up for yourself than for being treated badly.

When you do assert yourself you may find out that your fears are unwarranted.

If something feels wrong in the relationship for you then it is likely that your partner also feels that something is wrong. This means that there is something that needs to be talked about rather than suffering it and brushing it under the carpet.

That something has gone wrong in your relationship doesn't mean that something *is* wrong with you, your partner or the relationship.

Difficult behaviour –
don't take it personally, take time

When something your partner says or does evokes anger, guilt or distress in you it's easy to focus on those feelings within you. Maybe, you react with anger or tears, or cut off. That in turn may evoke similar feelings in your partner. If s/he reacts in the same way as you, you are in a vicious circle.

However, if you assume that neither of you wants the other to feel angry, guilty or distressed what are these rows about?

If, instead of reacting immediately to what your partner says or does, you take time to ask yourself what this says about the state your partner is in, you may find that your partner's words and actions are an expression of insecurity, distress or anxiety that has nothing to do with you.

If you have a sense of what lies behind your partner's behaviour then you can address this rather than reacting to the behaviour and so relate to each other instead of just to your own feelings.

In the way we relate to others and what we say to them we are also saying something about ourselves. If people behave in a way that is difficult for others this is often an indirect expression of difficulties in their lives.

We may want somebody special in our lives because we hope that this person will make things right for us. To some extent this is possible. A loving companion certainly enriches our life.

However, they cannot make up for something that's missing in you.

What a relationship cannot do for you

If you have low self-respect a relationship will not change that.

If you don't like yourself a relationship will not make you like yourself more. If you want a partner because you feel lonely on your own you might encounter a loneliness much more devastating when you have a row with you beloved or feel misunderstood and not seen.

No other person can make up for the love, care or respect that you are not prepared to give yourself. However, a partner may help you to accept that you deserve love, care and respect, just because you exist.

If you sense that your relationship to yourself is disturbed – maybe through your past or your childhood experiences - you could consider seeing a psychotherapist to help you develop a more secure relationship to yourself.

Taking responsibility for the relationship

It seems that in most relationships one partner takes more responsibility for the relationship than the other. However, if both partners can acknowledge full and sole responsibility not only for themselves but also for the relationship itself, then each will be taking a pro-active stance. They will not only consider what they want their partner to do to make things better, but what they can do to improve the relationship.

Yet even if only one partner takes responsibility for the relationship and for the other – and not just for their own needs – the relationship will endure.

> **The richer your own life is the more you can contribute to a relationship**

When we want a relationship we may think of a lot of different things we expect or wish for from being with a partner. Only one generation ago it was taken for granted that marriage and family life was the normal state for everybody, and that spinsters, bachelors and childless couples were creatures to be pitied. Values have changed since. More and more people chose not to have children, to live with a partner but not marry, to be with a partner for life but not live with her/him, or to stay single. Serial monogamy is now socially acceptable, as are sexual relationships between same sex partners or celibacy in a relationship.

With all these possibilities now open to us, we have to give serious thought to what we really want from a relationship. You may wish to raise a family, you may want somebody to share your life and grow old with, or you may want someone to take care of you, make you happy, give you status, or make you feel needed.

There are, of course, things you would normally need a partner for, like making children or truly sharing your life. There are others, however, which you can do on your own, like taking care of yourself, being happy on your own, feeling confident, having a full and rich life.

> **There are no 'bad' relationships,**
> **only people not good at relating**

The more you relate as who you are instead of who you think you should be - and the more you relate to your partner as they are and not as you think *they* should be - the more you'll enjoy the relationship, your partner and yourself.

Learning to relate happens through aware relating and through reflection and discussion between partners. The better you know your partner and yourself the better you will relate to each other. This will take time, so be patient with yourself and stay open to your partner.

.

EXAMPLE LIST

THIS IS MY IDEAL ....

<u>GENERAL FEATURES</u>

Male / female

Age range

Nationality

Race

Religion

Height

Figure

Hair colour

Colour of the eyes

Skin colour

Quality of the voice

Educational level

Employment status *(employed, self-employed, unemployed, free-lance, casual worker, independent income…, irrelevant)*

Location *(lives near, lives abroad, lives in Alaska, etc)*

Financial situation *(similar to yours, better off than you, average, rich …, irrelevant.)*

Social relations *(part of a community, gregarious, outgoing, good friend, loner, liked, quiet, prefers one-to-one, has good relationships with his/her family, no family, small/large social circle ....)*

Work related issues *(successful and respected in his/her work, loves and enjoys the work s/he does, doesn't work, works only occasionally, works from home, goes out to work, does the work that's important to him/her outside of a job..., irrelevant.)*

Interests *(current affairs/politics/ sports/ philosophy/ religion/ psychology/ handicrafts/DIY/ music/painting/ ballet/ theatre/ cars, home making ...)*

Active pursuits *(cooking, eating out, music, dancing, bowling, reading, going for walks, metal-detecting, sailing, travelling, TV, theatre, evenings at home with me and/or with friends etc)*

INNER QUALITIES
Only make positive statements and avoid formulations like 'not...' or 'not too...'
open, intellectual, intuitive, cool, stable, warm, intelligent, imaginative, rational, my kind of humour, emotionally aware and expressive, quiet, self contained, sensitive, creative, down to earth, loving, affectionate, well mannered, polite, considerate etc.

OTHER REQUIREMENTS

available, enjoys my company, loves me, unattached, children of his/her own, no children, well dressed, sexually attractive

Most people automatically assume that unless they find someone sexually attractive right from the start there is no chance of them being right for them, let alone becoming their 'ideal' partner. It may happen however, that your ideal partner doesn't initially seem sexually attractive to you in any way at all.

Don't worry about it!

Immediate physical attraction is a bonus but it can also lead you astray in your search for your ideal partner. Inner non-sexual attraction and closeness are more important. They can lead in their own time to strong sexual attraction and desire - even if it is not there to begin with.

After you've made your list write underneath:

This or something better will now come into my life in a harmonious and satisfying way.

Or you could reduce the list to 8 key qualities and playfully explore your feeling a bit more:

CHOOSING 8 KEY QUALITIES

You've done your list and know what kind of partner would be your ideal. Now chose the 8 inner qualities which are most important for you – like the following or any other combination which suits you

intelligent	sexy	zany
idealistic	sense of humour	free spirited
good listener	sociable	cheerful
empathic	adventurous	imaginative
creative	fun loving	open
spiritual	ambitious	warm hearted
politically aware	confident	non-judgemental
well read	well dressed	considerate

If you can, *invent a name* for your ideal partner which conveys both the inner and the physical qualities you are looking for. It could be a name that doesn't yet exist like Aborro or Amanuana, Perame or Suvunji – just sense and imagine your ideal partner and listen inwardly until a name comes to mind - one that fits your *feeling* of them. You could also invent a descriptive name like 'Gentle Hulk' or 'Butterfly Darling', or use a fictional name taken from a character in a novel or film. Using the name you have created write:

Dear (….) I now invite you to enter my life in a harmonious and satisfying way.

SUMMARY: THE EIGHT STEPS

Step 1: Embody a different you

Step 2: Visualise a different life

Step 3: Define your relationship

Step 4: Make a list

Step 5: Review and change your list

Step 6: State your intent

Step 7: Affirm your intent

Step 8: Let go

APPENDIX by Peter Wilberg

30 REFLECTIONS ON RELATING AND RELATIONSHIPS

1. Relationships are all about actively *relating* to others – not just passively waiting to see how things turn out.

2. Ideal relationships arise from taking a real *interest* in another person and in relating to the real person - not an ideal image of them.

3. If your *only* interest is in whether a partner meets your own needs, ideals and expectations there can be no real relationship at all.

4. There are no 'bad' relationships, only people not good at relating - or not genuinely interested in the real person they are relating to.

5. If you are not interested in or don't want to relate to your partner's fears or anxieties, weaknesses or idiosyncrasies, difficult or dark sides, then you are not interested in relating to the real person – the whole person.

6. There is nothing 'black and white' about any relationship. It is in its grey areas and shadows that its richest colours can be found.

7. The richer your own life is – the more you understand about relationships, the deeper your interest in all people, and the broader your interests outside the relationship - the more you can contribute *to* a relationship.

8. For a relationship to last at least one partner must take responsibility for the relationship itself – and not just their own needs within it.

9. A partner can't make up for what you are not or turn you into someone else. Nor can you turn your partner into someone else.

10. On the other hand, your partner may offer you a valuable mirror of parts of yourself you don't acknowledge, reveal or live out to the full.

11. You do not need to hide or sacrifice any part of yourself in a relationship – for how can there be a relationship if you are not relating from your *whole* self?

12. Be assured that any ideal partner will be someone wanting a relationship that works and lasts as much as you do.

13. Real people will never quite fit ideal expectations – or not do so in quite the way you expect - and yet they may still be ideal partners in ways you don't recognise.

14. If something feels wrong for you in the relationship then something probably feels wrong for your partner too. The fact that something goes wrong *in* a relationship doesn't mean there is anything wrong *with* the relationship – or with yourself, or with your partner.

15. Problems or difficulties in relationships are opportunities and challenges to learn to relate and communicate more deeply and intimately.

16. Real intimacy and inner closeness in relationships cannot be created through sexual intimacy. On the other hand, sexual intimacy can arise from and express real inner closeness and intimacy.

17. It is not just similarities but differences that make relationships rich and fertile. 'Similarities are delightful. Differences are enriching.' A relationship without differences, though it may seem to cause less difficulties, is like a relationship with a mirror image of yourself – in other words no relationship at all.

18. 'A difficult person is a person in difficulty'. Things you find 'difficult' about your partner may express difficulties they experience in themselves – or your own difficulty in acknowledging them.

19. Don't always 'take it personally' if your partner gets upset with you. They may either have good reasons – or they are upset for reasons that have nothing to do with you personally.

20. No one who fully accepts themselves fears 'rejection' - or needs to reject another just because of difficulties they have with them.

21. No one can *make* another person feel a certain way - good or bad, happy or sad, angry or depressed. If you *believe* that another person has 'made' you feel upset, then that belief alone – and not the other person – will upset you and make you feel helpless, angry or depressed.

22. Relating means taking responsibility for one's own feelings. That means affirming them *as* one's own feeling, finding ways of responding to them *in* oneself and sharing them with others – not blaming our feelings *on* others.

23. Though your ideal partner can help you through the difficulties, conflicts, stresses and boredom of life, they can't make life itself ideal.

24. People change – for better or worse. To maintain a relationship means helping each other to change for the better - and learning to relate to the *new* person your partner may have become.

25. If you feel your partner has changed in a significant and positive way it's catch up time for you – a creative challenge to learn from them and to change yourself – not a reason for feeling yourself or the relationship threatened.

26. Every human being needs solitude - time and space for themselves. That is why in any long-term relationship there is a natural rhythm and alternation between periods of solitude and togetherness. Withdrawal into solitude is not withdrawal from the relationship but a most basic condition for recreating togetherness and sustaining relationships.

27. If you do not create times and spaces for solitude – for 'coming back to yourself' - how can you fully relate to your partner from yourself? If you do not allow your partner spaces and times to 'withdraw' into themselves at times, how can they 'come back to themselves' and be fully there for you?

28. Fear of our own space and time being 'invaded', the belief that solitude needs to be sacrificed to the relationship – or failure to affirm and protect our needs for withdrawal into solitude – these are some of the biggest obstacles to entering into and maintaining a relationship, particularly one that involves living together with a partner.

29. One of the greatest and most healing gifts a relationship can bring is the possibility it grants of being alone *with* another – of having another human being who one can just *be with* in complete silence – without needing to talk or do something.

30. The most truly 'ideal' relationship is one in which one can enjoy being with another human being and feeling the comfort of their silent presence, whilst at the same time being fully with and 'alone' ('all-one' and 'at one') with oneself. Relationship and aloneness, togetherness and solitude are not opposites.

Karin Heinitz has worked as a counsellor and psychotherapist in private practice for more than 30 years. She lives in a small coastal town in the South-East of England.

Her main interest outside of work is music and The New Yoga (www.thenewyoga.org).

She has also published

Tantric Poetry – My Lord of the Living Light, New Yoga Publications, 2010